The Best Little Networking Guide

By Marc Zirogiannis

Zirogiannis, Marc
The Best Little Networking Guide

ISBN: 978-1-365-70081-1

44 PAGES

Inquiries or additional information contact:

Marc A. Zirogiannis
Email: mmasuperstore@gmail.com

ABOUT THE AUTHOR

Marc Zirogiannis holds a B.A. from Long Island University and a *Juris Doctor* from Hofstra University's School of Law. Mr. Zirogiannis is a world renowned Business Development Consultant. Mr. Zirogiannis has practiced the martial arts for over 25 years and earned a [2nd] Dan under the supervision of Grandmaster Yeon Hwan Park in Levittown, New York. He is a Taekwondo Referee with 25 years of experience. He has published several prior books on a variety of subjects, and, is currently the lead correspondent for an international Tae Kwon Do print publication. He lectures, and has written numerous books, on a variety of topics, including suicide prevention, business development, and matters of the martial arts.

INTRODUCTION

Networking is defined as *Creating a group of acquaintances and associates and keeping it active through regular communication for mutual benefit. Networking is based on the question "How can I help?" and not with "What can I get?"*

Most business owners view Networking as a specific component of a larger, business marketing plan. This is not accurate and this approach "leaves money on the table" every time. Networking should not be a component of a stand-alone business, marketing plan. It should be an intrinsic part of the businesses' operational existence. Every action a business owner takes and everything they do should have an eye on using Networking to create a stronger, more loyal, business base and as the building blocks of business longevity.

This work is the product of a series of educational and inspirational lectures given by me to business networking organizations over the last few years. Each component chapter was the basis of an extensive lecture on the underlying topic. It is designed as an easy to use, easy to integrate starting place for understanding the nature of Networking and its place as a component of business success.

The goal is for business owners to use this work to commence a journey along the path of business Networking and success.

5 QUOTES ON ACHIEVING SUCCESS

1.   "I never dreamed about success. I worked for it."
– **Estee Lauder**

2.   "Don't spend so much time trying to choose the perfect opportunity, that you miss the right opportunity." – **Michael Dell**

3.   "Above all, you want to create something you are proud of. That's always been my philosophy of business. I can honestly say that I have never gone into any business purely to make money. If that is the sole motive, then I believe you are better off doing nothing."
– **Richard Branson**

4.   "It has been my observation that most people get ahead during the time that others waste." – **Henry Ford**

5.   "Time is your most important resource. You can do so much in ten minutes. Ten minutes; once gone is gone for good." – **Ingvar Kamprad IKEA**

SIX RULES OF SUCCESS

(From Arnold Schwarzenegger)

1. Trust Yourself
   a. Ask yourself, "Who do you want to be?"

2. Break Some Rules
   a. Think Outside the Box.

3. Don't Be Afraid to Fail
   a. Don't be paralyzed by fear.

4. Ignore the Naysayers
   a. Tell yourself "Yes, You Can!"

5. Work Like Hell
   a. Never let anyone outwork you. While you are partying someone else is working hard.

6. Give Something Back
   a. Always find the time and a way.

FINDING TIME TO NETWORK

(from Hyrum W. Smith-CEO Franklin Quest)

1. You control your life by controlling your time
2. Your governing values are the foundation of personal success
3. When your daily activities express your governing values, you achieve success
4. To reach any significant goal you must leave your comfort zone
5. Consistent daily planning leverages time and increases focus

The underlying theme is that success in networking is not the product of accidental or incidental interaction. It is the product of arranging your schedule to make this an integral part of your schedule and business.

HOW TO CHOOSE A NETWORKING GROUP

1. Does this networking group serve your target audience?

2. Does this group have members who ARE your audience – people who know or serve your industry or company targets?

3. How much time does active membership in each group take?

4. How often do they meet?

5. How big is your personal commitment?

RELATIONSHIP MARKETING- PART-1

(Courtesy of marketing-schools.org)

Relationship marketing is about forming <u>long-term relationships</u> with customers. Rather than trying to encourage a one-time sale, relationship marketing tries to foster customer loyalty by providing exemplary products and services. This is different than most normal advertising practices that focus on a single transaction; watch ad A and buy product B.

Relationship marketing, by contrast, is usually not linked to a single product or offer. **It involves a company refining the way they do business in order to maximize the value of that relationship for the customer.**

Some Practices:

Relationship Marketing Best Practices

- Solicit feedback from customers and incorporate it into the company's business practices.
- Use any and all social media outlets to connect with customers.
- Leverage the value of warm leads –

customers who have already expressed an interest in the company.

- Maintain a high customer satisfaction rate in all areas of the company.
- Make an effort to inform customers how much they are appreciated.

RELATIONSHIP MARKETING-PART 2

"What if businesses decided to inform, rather than promote? You know that expression 'If you give a man a fish, you feed him for a day; if you teach a man to fish, you feed him for a lifetime?' The same is true for marketing: If you sell something, you make a customer today; if you help someone, you make a customer for life. In every business category, one company will commit to being the best teacher, and the most helpful. And that company will be rewarded with attention, sales, loyalty and advocacy by consumers who are sick to death of being sold, sold, sold."

Jay Baer, author of Youtility

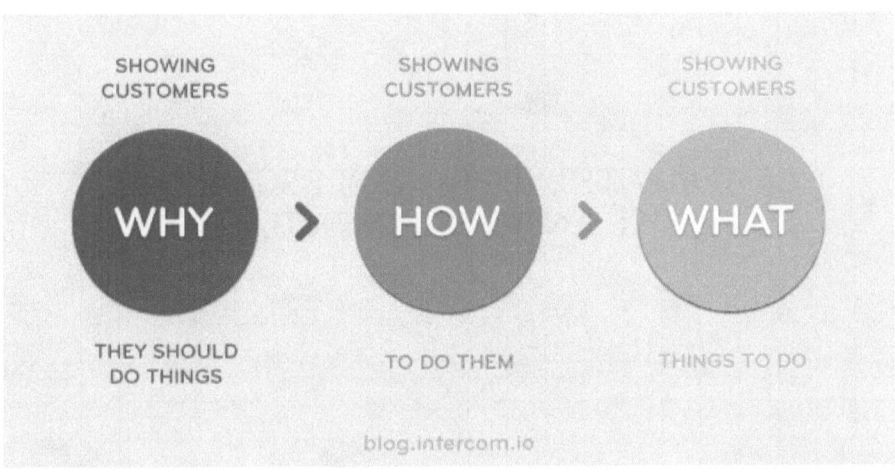

RELATIONSHIP MARKETING-Part 3

YOUR NETWORKING GROUP IS YOUR
RELATIONSHIP MARKETING INCUBATOR:

HOW?

- We do NOT focus on the "One and Done" point of sale
- We teach others in our group about the value of our business
- We develop long term relationships which transcend our weekly meetings

APPLY THESE PRINCIPLES TO YOUR
CLIENT/CUSTOMER BASE

CUSTOMER REFERRAL STRATEGIES-
PART 1

(From JoAnne Black, author of <u>Pick Up The Damn Phone</u>)

1. **Understand what you're asking**. When you ask for a referral, you are actually asking your source to put his or her reputation on the line in order to endorse you as a person worthy of a colleague's attention. It's a big deal so treat it accordingly.

2. **Earn trust first**. You are wasting your time asking for a referral when you first contact a prospective customer. If somebody hasn't bought from you and confirmed you are worth a colleagues' attention, you aren't going to get a useful referral.

3. **Be specific about who you need**. Rather than asking for "somebody who needs my services," define (for your source) the type of person and company who's most likely to need what you have to offer. Better yet, have a specific individual in mind. (Hint: use LinkedIn.)

Customer Referral Strategies- Part 2

(From JoAnne Black, author of <u>Pick Up The Damn Phone</u>)

4. Ask for an action not a contact. Rather than simply asking for name, phone and email, ask your source to call or email the prospect. Make it clear what you'd like your source to say and confirm that your source will be comfortable saying it.

5. Get a commitment for a confirmation. Ask your source to get back to you (or copy you on the email) so that you're certain your source has taken the action that you've requested... before you follow up on the referral.

6. Immediately thank your source. When your source agrees to take action on your behalf, offer your profuse thanks and appreciation, *before your source has taken any action!* This is not only appropriate but reminds the source to actually take the action.

CUSTOMER REFERRAL STRATEGIES- PART 3

(From JoAnne Black, author of <u>Pick Up The Damn Phone</u>)

7. Follow up on the referral. Since your source has already endorsed you, you've got the inside track. Use it well.

8. Thank your source again. After you've followed up on the referral, call or email with your thanks and a brief status report, like "You were right; Fred is a great guy."

9. If you make a sale, thank your source again. If the referral generates a sale, send another thank you to your source. This is not only appropriate, but also encourages the source to continue to refer other prospects!

3 Networking Success Tips

Strategically plan your networking.

Think about people who would be good contacts for your business. If you're not a financial expert, develop a strong relationship with an accountant. If you need to reach parents, network at school events. Set aside time every month for networking -- try having lunch with one new person a week or go to three networking events every month.

Prepare for networking.

Before a networking meeting, make sure you have plenty of business cards. Do some research on the people who may attend so you have conversation-starters. Be a good listener when meeting new people.

Follow-up after meeting someone.

Send a card, leave a message, or send an E-mail telling the person it was great meeting them. Ask if you can put them on your contact list and send them information about your company. Regularly send articles or other information that may be helpful to them.

Networking IS not cold calling

(from Derek Singleton)

1. Cold Calling is very labor intensive.

2. Cold Calling has a very low rate of conversion.

3. Consumers and Businesses are tuned out to Cold Calls.

4. Regulations have made Cold Calling harder, more expensive, and, potentially, legally complex.

5. Greater return on investment from relationship marketing firm or networking group than using Cold Calling method.

9 NETWORKING BENEFITS
(PART 1)

(from Kim Baird)

1. **Increased Business**
   a. Higher Quality Referrals
   b. Greater Conversion Rate
   c. Pre-Qualified Leads

2. **Opportunities That May Arise**
   a. Joint ventures
   b. Partnerships
   c. Speaking engagements
   d. Business Sales and Purchases

3. **Connections**
   a. Concentration of good connections
   b. Built in "Council of Experts"

9 NETWORKING BENEFITS

(PART 2)

(from Kim Baird)

1. **Advice**
    a. Broad spectrum of Advisors
    b. Experts in their field

2. **Raising Your Profile**
    a. Visibility within your group
    b. Opportunities to visit other Networking Events
    c. SEO Optimization

3. **Positive Influence**
    a. Networkers are ambitious
    b. Networkers are motivated
    c. Networkers are a positive influence on growth

9 Networking benefits

(part 3)

(from Kim Baird)

1. **Increased Confidence**
   a. Chances to practice your sales pitch
   b. Get comfortable talking about you

2. **Satisfaction of Helping Others**
   a. You become part of a problem solving team

3. **Friendship**
   a. Relationships that transcend the group meetings

3 NETWORKING TIPS TO ADD GROWTH TO YOUR BUSINESS

(from Gay Gaddis)

1. Don't get bogged down in your own industry groups. The best leads may come for people in other industries that have a need for your skills.

2. Building relationships takes time. Don't get discouraged if leads don't flow immediately. With the building of trust and an understanding of what you do more and sounder leads will follow.

3. Get involved in a big way. You can't be half involved and expect people to see you as a serious player. Show a real and honest commitment and people will respond accordingly.

NETWORKING DON'TS

(from Catriona Pollard)

1. **DON'T-** Go with your friend or you will spend time catching up rather than meeting other people. Think of this as a business meeting, not a social event.

2. **DON'T-** Stare around the room when you talking with people. Make eye contact. Make sure the person you are speaking to recognizes you are paying attention to them.

3. **DON'T-** Try to do a hard sell; networking is about getting to know people. These are not cold calls; they are relationship-building opportunities. They are investments in a future business opportunity.

4. **DON'T-** Say you will follow up with people and not bother. Not following up not only misses an opportunity, but also entrenches your reputation as unreliable. If you don't follow up with the source you will, likely, not follow up with the referral.

Top 5 Reasons Businesses fail

(From *INC. Magazine*, July 2014)

1. Failure to market online.

2. Failing to listen to their customers. It is not 1972. Get with the times.

3. Failing to leverage future growth. Don't always focus on today. Spend a little time every day thinking about tomorrow, next week, next month…..

4. Failing to adapt (and grow) when the market changes. Traditionalism is important; however, it must be balanced with sensible change and adaptation.

5. Failing to track and measure your marketing efforts. Don't expect to take a blind approach to your business and succeed. Have metrics for growth. Track sales leads. Examine spending. Measure risk vs. reward continuously.

5 WAY TO BE MORE PRODUCTIVE AT WORK

In a recent article from the **Huffington Post** entitled, "**5 Surprising Things Ways To Be More Productive At Work**" some of the following non-monetary suggestions were made to improve the workplace environment and productivity of American workers. These included:

1.   Introduce Plant Life into the Work Environment- Studies have shown that plants in the workplace create a more pleasant and productive environment. Any type of foliage will do. It is best to suit them to the environment, lighting, and the workers' abilities to care for them when choosing plant types. Dead plants defeat the concept.

2.   Temperature Control- Creating a comfortable temperature through thermostat, or clothing, adjustments is vital to productivity. One study even found that typists made less errors at 71 degrees F than at lower temperatures. The key is finding a comfortable temperature that works for the whole staff. Fighting over the thermostat is not conducive to a healthy work environment.

3.   Save Your Exercise for the Gym- Whether it is to save time, or because workers are under the impression that physical activity during the conduct of business was beneficial, exercise on the job, actually, decreased worker productivity according to one analysis. Workers that ran on a treadmill while conducting business did neither activity, particularly, well.

4. Ambient Lighting and Noise- Low lighting and some level of noise have tested as positive to worker productivity. While blocking out all noise may seem like a good way to concentrate, it seems that the complete absence of noise is not the optimal environment for being productive.

5. Lose the Angles- If you have any say in the furniture in your work environment it seems that studies reveal that softer, rounded edges to furniture are more conducive to productivity than sharp, hard edges like conventional business furniture. An expert in design may come in handy here.

13 STEPS TO BUSINESS SUCCESS

(From Napoleon Hill)

1. **Desire:** You have to want it. Without desire everything else is just perfunctory and everyone will notice.

2. **Faith:** Believe you can achieve. How do you expect others to believe in you in you don't believe in yourself.

3. **The Power of Suggestion:** Positive thought. Negative thoughts lead to negative action. Read **The Secret.**

4. **Specialized Knowledge:** Always be learning. The more specialized your knowledge the more valuable and unique your skill set is.

5. **Imagination:** Be Creative. Stand out from the crowd.

6. **Organized Planning:** Dreams Don't Equal Actions. You must have an execution plan and you must track your progress along the journey.

7. **Decision:** Be Decisive-Don't Overthink. Commit

to your decisions and work to insure their success.

8. **Persistence:** Do Not Quit. Failure is just a result you didn't intend.   If the result is wrong change the pathway to achieve the result you intended.

9.   **Power of the Master Mind:** Surround yourself with the best. Your parents with right. You are judged and influenced by the company you keep.

10.   **Choose a compatible partner.** Support at home is invaluable. Choose someone who understands and cares.

11. **The Subconscious Mind:** Master positivity and dismiss negative emotions.

12. **The Brain:** Associate with other smart people and learn from them. "2+2=6". Smart people have a way of inspiring and motivating each other to new heights.

13. **The Sixth Sense:** Trust your gut. Intuition is a GIFT from God.   Trust yourself. Trust your instincts.

*After surveying 500 millionaires in 1937!

CLIENT RETENTION VS. ACQUISITION COST ANALYSIS

(From Our Social Times)

From A 2013 Survey of US Companies

1. 70% of US companies surveyed say it's cheaper to retain a customer than acquire a new one and 49% say that, pound for pound, they achieve better ROI (Return on Investment) by investing in relationship marketing over acquisition marketing.

YET

2. 70% of Companies have no specific protocol in place for customer retention

  a. Reasons Cited:
     i. "lack of resources",
     ii. "not clearly defined strategy",
     iii. "technology limitations"
     iv. "lack of single customer view".

So when analyzing your allocation of financial and time resources keep these numbers in mind.

RAVING FANS BY KEN BLANCHARD- A MUST READ

Here are the salient highlights of the book to consider:

1.   Only 4% of all businesses survive for 10 years-WOW;

2.   Success is a product of:

     a. **Innovation- "Finding a better way to meet your client's needs than anyone"**

     b. **Marketing-   "The Best Product Doesn't Always Win"**

3.   **A QUESTION TO ASK EVERY DAY** –"Who are my customers and what do they need?"

4.   It's not enough to say you are the best. You must develop a romantic relationship with your client that makes breaking up painful.   You need to be an integral part of their business plan and their success. You need to be interwoven into their fabric and the fabric of their business.

5.   Failure to anticipate and adapt will lead to EXTINCTION. This is for certain.

6.   It is not the 5% of your clients that complain, or the 5% of your clients that compliment you that you need to focus on -it is the silent 90%. Their silence means you are NOTHING TO THEM.   They are all subject to walking away without concern.   Focus on the silent 90%.   Turn them from silent bystanders to your sales army.   Convert a greater percentage of them to RAVING FANS and the referrals and $$$$$$ will follow. This concept is lost to most business owners.

ADDRESSING CUSTOMER COMPLAINTS

1. Read the entire complaint before doing anything.
2. Avoid the impulse to respond immediately and emotionally.
3. Address every communication: Good or Bad
   a. Email
   b. Call
   c. Send Out Cards
   d. Posted Response
4. Urban Meyer, the Great Ohio State Football Coach, is a great organizational and motivational speaker.
   One concept from his recent book, <u>Above the Line,</u> that I love-
   In problem solving the most destructive thing we can do is engage in what he calls the B,C,D's.

   Never: ***B****lame,* ***C****omplain, or* ***D****efend*

5. Unemotionally breakdown the essence of the complaint.
   a. Why did they take the time to complain?
   b. What is the real issue?
   c. What could you have done differently to avoid this complaint?
   d. Are their elements of this complaint that ring true from other comments or complaints?
   e. What was good about the contact?

6. Respond Appropriately
   a. ***THANK THE PERSON FIRST ALWAYS***
   b. Address the issues without engaging in the B,C, D's
   c. Avoid the use of the term "BUT"
   d. Never engage in insulting or inflammatory communication
   e. Never attack the complainant
   f. Do not get personal
   g. Do not engage in negotiation or "bribery"
   h. Invite the party to give you another opportunity to rectify the matter
7. If the matter can not be resolved then disengage- DO NOT ESCALATE
8. Take whatever administrative remedies you deem appropriate
9. LEARN FROM THE EXPERIENCE.

CUSTOMER & CLIENT RETENTION TOOLS

(Courtesy of marketing WIZDOM)

1. Frequent Communications Calendar

Avoid losing your customers by building relationships and keeping in touch using a rolling calendar of communications. This is a programmed sequence of letters, events, phone calls, "thank you's", special offers, follow-ups, magic moments, and cards or notes with a personal touch etc. that occur constantly and automatically at defined points in the pre-sales, sales and post-sales process. People not only respond to this positively, they really appreciate it because they feel valued and important. It acknowledges them, keeps them informed, offsets post-purchase doubts, reinforces the reason they're doing business with you and makes them feel part of your business so that they want to come back again and again.

2. Product or service integrity

Long-term success and customer retention belongs to those who do not take ethical shortcuts. There must always be total **consistency** between what you say and do and what your customers experience. The design, build quality, reliability and serviceability of your product or service must be of the standard your customers want, need and expect. <u>Service integrity is also demonstrated by the way you handle the small things, as well as the large</u>. Customers will be attracted to you if you are open and honest with them, care for them, take a genuine interest in them, don't let them down and practice what you preach ... and they will avoid you if you don't.

3. Measure lifetime value

There's a vast difference between the one-off profit you might make on an average sale, which ignores the bigger picture, and the total aggregate profit your average customer represents over the lifetime of their business relationship with you. Once you recognize how much combined profit a customer represents to your business when they purchase from you again and again, over the months, years or decades, you'll realize the critical importance of taking good care of your customers. And because you'll understand just how much time, effort and expense you can afford to invest in retaining that customer, you'll be in control of your marketing expenditure

4. A complaint is a gift

96 percent of dissatisfied customers don't complain. They just walk away, and you'll never know why. That's because they often don't know how to complain, or can't be bothered, or are too frightened, or don't

believe it'll make any difference. Whilst they may not tell you what's wrong, they will certainly tell plenty of others. A system for unearthing complaints can therefore be the lifeblood of your business, because customers who complain are giving you a gift, they're still talking to you, they're giving you another opportunity to return them to a state of satisfaction and delight them and the manner in which you respond gives you another chance to show what you're made of and create even greater customer loyalty.

5. Courtesy system

A powerful system that improves the interpersonal skills of your team and changes the spirit of your organization. It involves speaking to colleagues politely and pleasantly, without sarcasm or parody, and treating them at least as well as you would want them to treat your customers. This will help your team to feel worthwhile and important, which makes for pleasant social contacts at work. It also motivates them to provide extraordinary service, encourages them to be consistently pleasant in all of their dealings and to relate to customers in a warm, human and natural manner. This results in better, warmer, stronger, more trusting relationships and longer-term bonds with your customers.

FIRST THINGS FIRST BY STEVEN COVEY- THE ORGANIZATIONAL BIBLE

	Urgent	Not Urgent
Important	**I** ACTIVITIES: Crises Pressing problems Deadline-driven projects	**II** ACTIVITIES: Prevention Relationship building Recreation New opportunities
Not Important	**III** ACTIVITIES: Interruptions Some phone calls Some mail Some meetings Popular activities	**IV** ACTIVITIES: Trivia Some mail Some phone calls Time wasters Pleasure activities

-Quadrant I activities are things that are important and urgent, that is driven by both the clock and the compass. Examples of Quadrant I activities include deadline-driven projects, real crises, and pressing problems. The key to understanding this quadrant is that activities aren't considered Quadrant I just because they are urgent to someone else. The activities have to be important in terms of "greater values.

-Quadrant II activities are tasks that are important but not urgent, that is, driven by the compass and not the clock. Examples of Quadrant II activities include long range planning, preparation and activities that build relationships and community.

-Quadrant III activities are not important but are urgent that is, driven completely by clock and not at all by the compass. Examples of Quadrant II activities include interruptions and dealing with other people's emergencies.

-Quadrant IV activities are not important and not urgent, that is, driven by neither the compass nor the clock. Examples of these type of activities include, busywork, unneeded paperwork and escape activities such as watching reality television."

"In order to really feel some kind of basic satisfaction with life, Covey states, people need to attend more to Quadrant II activities. However, there is a natural human tendency to mood manage with Quadrant III activities. This natural human tendency is reinforced by the pace of modern life. Managing a crisis or attending to some perceived emergency gives a hit of adrenaline that is satisfying short term and also temporarily distracts from negative emotions like boredom or existential sadness."

TEXTING TIPS FOR BUSINESS

1. Be sure texting is an acceptable means of communication to recipient.

2. Refrain from texting outside of business hours.

3. Avoid Acronyms and Abbreviations.

4. Use sparingly.   Do not replace phone calls or emails in business with lengthy texts.

5. Do not text others while on networking appointments with new prospects.

6. Do not rely on unconfirmed texts to change or schedule appointments.

7. Do not text, email, and call the person about the same matter. Choose one form of communication.

3 Keys to enduring difficult economic times

(From Gravitational Marketing)

#1: Differentiate

Discover what is unique about you, your product or service, your process, your strengths and weaknesses and exploit them to their fullest extent.

#2: Innovate

By innovating you show freshness, confidence and give the community a bit of hope, encouragement and exhilaration.

#3: Connect

Your goal is to become regarded by your customers as more than just a huckster of some goods or services, and instead to position yourself as a helper to their family. Someone who makes their quality of life better, their decision making process easier, and their minds more informed.

BUSINESS LESSONS FROM THE DALAI LAMA

(Courtesy of His Holiness the 14th Dalai lama of Tibet)

1. Love what you do, and do it the whole way.

2. When you lose, don't lose the lesson.

3. Don't let a little dispute injure a great relationship.

4. Open your arms to change, but don't let go of your values.

5. Follow the three Rs:
   a. Respect Yourself
   b. Respect Others
   c. Be Responsible

6. Share Your Knowledge
   a. Of all the things you wear to work your expression is the most important.

SALES STATISTICS

48% OF SALES PEOPLE NEVER FOLLOW UP WITH A PROSPECT
25% OF SALES PEOPLE MAKE A SECOND CONTACT AND STOP
12% OF SALES PEOPLE ONLY MAKE THREE CONTACTS AND STOP
ONLY 10% OF SALES PEOPLE MAKE MORE THAN THREE CONTACTS

2% OF SALES ARE MADE ON THE FIRST CONTACT
3% OF SALES ARE MADE ON THE SECOND CONTACT

5% OF SALES ARE MADE ON THE 3RD CONTACT
10% OF SALES ARE MADE ON THE 4TH CONTACT
80% OF SALES ARE MADE ON THE 5TH TO 12TH CONTACT

FACT: 95% OF SALES
Are Made AFTER the 3rd-12th Contact

Do You Have a System to Stay in Touch?

NETWORK EDUCATION

GOAL SETTING FOR A NEW YEAR

Goal Setting is important to growth and success in business.

Some tips:

1. Set realistic and attainable goals. Do not set yourself up for failure.

2. Write down a list of your goals for the year and keep it close.

3. Design a plan to achieving your goals.

4. Your goals should have two components:
   a. Make you a little bit scared or nervous
   b. Make you VERY Excited

CONCLUSION

Networking success does not happen overnight. It takes time and effort to make Networking an intrinsic part of your business operations. Use this work as a starting place for commencing the journey. Don't get discouraged. This is a journey that requires patience but the payoff is a vibrant series of relationships that will become annuities in building and sustaining your business well into the future.